ABOUT THE AUTHOR

Neil Ardley has written a number of innovative nonfiction books for children, including *The Eyewitness Guide to Music*. He also worked closely with David Macaulay on *The Way Things Work*. In addition to being a well-known author in the fields of science, technology, and music, he is an accomplished musician who composes and performs both jazz and electronic music. He lives in Derbyshire, England, with his wife and daughter.

Project Editor Linda Martin
Art Editor Peter Bailey
Designer Mark Regardsoe
Photography Dave King
Created by Dorling Kindersley Limited, London

Library of Congress Cataloging-in-Publication Data
Ardley, Neil.
The science book of sound/Neil Ardley.—1st U.S. ed.
p. cm.
"Gulliver books."
Summary: Simple experiments demonstrate basic principles of sound and music.
ISBN 0-15-200579-X
1. Sound—Juvenile literature. 2. Music—Acoustics and physics—Juvenile literature. [1. Sound—Experiments. 2. Music—Acoustics and physics. 3. Experiments.] I. Title.
QC225.5.A69 1991
534—dc20   90-48029

Printed in Belgium by Proost
First U.S. edition 1991
A B C D E

THE SCIENCE BOOK OF SOUND

Neil Ardley

Property of

HBJ

Gulliver Books

Harcourt Brace Jovanovich, Publishers

San Diego   New York   London

What is sound?

Sounds are nothing more than tiny movements of the air. You cannot feel these movements, but your ears detect them and your brain turns them into sounds that you can recognize. Every day you hear sounds made by people, animals, wind, and machines. The sounds you make with your voice allow you to communicate with other people. Animals also use sounds as a way of communicating with one another.

Sound signals
We often use sounds as signals. Blowing a whistle in a game can mean "stop" or "go."

Sea songs
Whales in the ocean "sing" to each other. One whale can hear the call of another as far as 800 kilometers (500 miles) away!

The speed of sound
The sound of this balloon bursting does not take long to travel through the air. Sound moves through air at a speed of 340 meters (1,115 feet) per second.

Sound pictures
The picture on this screen shows an unborn baby inside its mother. The picture was made using sounds that are too high-pitched for us to hear. These sounds are called "ultrasound."

Making music
Music is great fun. You can make musical sounds with homemade instruments like these.

⚠ This is a warning symbol. It appears within an experiment next to a step that requires caution. When you see this symbol, ask an adult for help.

Be a safe scientist
Follow all the instructions carefully and always use caution, especially with glass, scissors, and electricity.

Never put anything into your ears, eyes, or mouth. Remember that loud noises can bother other people. Please be considerate when doing these experiments.

Squawkers and screechers

You can make some strange sounds without using your voice. All you need is a piece of plastic or a straw. With practice, these can sound like the cries of wild animals!

You will need:

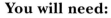
Drinking straw

Strip of thin plastic

Scissors

1 Hold the strip of plastic tightly between your thumbs and the heels of your hands.

2 Blow hard across the strip. It makes a loud screeching sound.

Try bending your thumbs as you blow.

1 Press one end of the straw flat. Cut the sides to form a point.

Keep the end of the straw flat.

Try two or more straws at once. Cut them to different lengths.

2 Put the pointed end of the straw in your mouth and blow hard. Out comes a weird squawk!

Balloon sounds

Make a loud shrieking noise with a balloon and you will see how rapid movements, or "vibrations," make sound.

You will need:

Balloon pump

Balloon

1 Pump up the balloon. Pinch the neck to stop the air escaping.

2 Grip the neck of the balloon and stretch it. The balloon makes a sound as the air escapes.

The escaping air makes the neck move quickly back and forth, or "vibrate." Sounds occur when things vibrate.

Tighten or loosen your grip on the balloon to see how many different sounds you can make.

Human sounds
Vocal cords in your throat vibrate and make sounds as the air from your lungs flows over them. Your mouth and lips form these sounds into words.

Sound detector

How do we hear the sounds around us? You can make a plastic drum and see how it detects sound. Your ears detect sounds in the same way.

You will need:

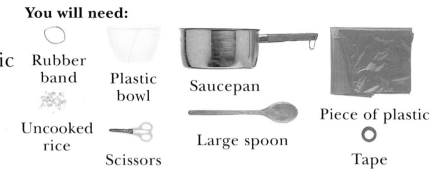

Rubber band

Plastic bowl

Saucepan

Piece of plastic

Uncooked rice

Scissors

Large spoon

Tape

1 Cut the piece of plastic so that it is a few inches bigger than the top of the bowl.

2 Stretch the plastic tightly over the bowl and secure it with a rubber band.

3 Tape the plastic down to keep it taut. This is your drum.

Stretch the plastic as tightly as possible across the bowl.

4 Sprinkle a few grains of rice on top of the drum.

5 Hold the saucepan near the drum and hit it sharply with the spoon. The grains of rice jump up and down.

When you hit the saucepan, it vibrates.

The sound travels through the air to the plastic drum, which also vibrates.

The vibrations cause the rice to jump.

If you look from the side, you can see the rice jumping up and down quite clearly.

Inside the ear

Inside each of your ears is a thin sheet of skin called the eardrum. Sounds are directed to your eardrum by your outer ear. When they reach the eardrum, it vibrates. The inner ear transforms these vibrations into signals that the brain then translates into the sounds you hear.

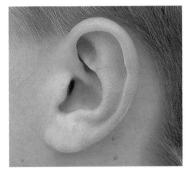

Traveling sound waves

Sounds travel through the air by spreading out in invisible waves, similar to the ripples on a pond. These waves are called "sound waves." Fire a sound wave at a target and see sound waves in action.

You will need:

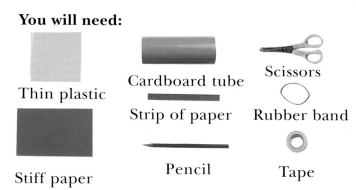

Thin plastic

Cardboard tube

Scissors

Stiff paper

Strip of paper

Rubber band

Pencil

Tape

1 Use the tube to trace a circle on the piece of paper.

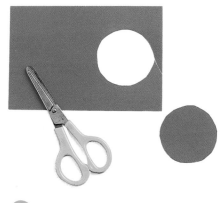

2 Cut out the circle.

3 Make a hole in the center of the circle with the pencil.

4 Tape the circle firmly to one end of the tube.

5 Fold the plastic over the other end of the tube, and secure it with the rubber band.

6 Make a fold in the paper strip and tape one end to a flat surface so that the other end sticks up.

The tap makes the air inside the tube vibrate and a sound wave travels down the tube.

7 Position the end of the tube so the hole is directly above the paper strip. Sharply tap the other end of the tube.

The air moves back and forth as the sound wave passes, shaking the paper strip.

The sound wave is pushed through the hole.

Sliding snow
A loud sound can cause an avalanche. The sound waves disturb the snow and start a mass of snow suddenly sliding down the mountain.

Paper noisemaker

You can make a loud bang with just a sheet of paper! This will show you how a sudden movement can send a powerful sound wave rushing through the air. You can use your noisemaker to surprise and startle your friends.

You will need:

Sheet of paper about
30 x 40 cm (12 x 16 in)

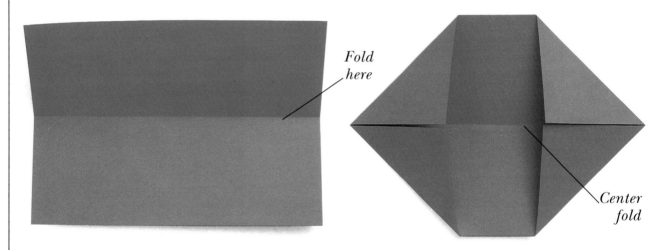

Fold here

Center fold

1 Fold the longest edges of the paper together. Crease firmly, then unfold it.

2 Fold down each of the four corners to the first center fold.

Fold here and open out.

Crease firmly.

3 Fold the paper in half along the first center fold.

4 Fold the paper in half again and then open it.

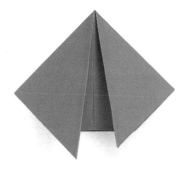

6 Fold the paper back to make a triangle. The noisemaker is now ready.

5 Fold down the two top corners.

7 Grip the noisemaker firmly by the two top corners. Snap it down sharply with a quick flick of the wrist. You should hear a loud bang!

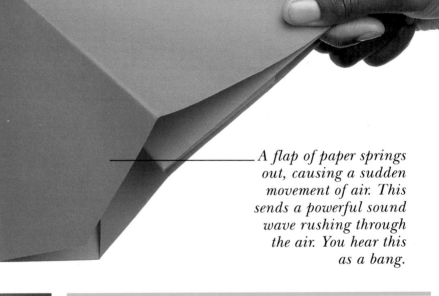

A flap of paper springs out, causing a sudden movement of air. This sends a powerful sound wave rushing through the air. You hear this as a bang.

Thunderclap

In a thunderstorm, a flash of lightning makes a powerful sound wave spread out through the air. When this sound wave reaches our ears, we hear a thunderclap.

Talking string

Besides traveling through air, sounds can also travel through objects. You can demonstrate this by making a simple telephone. This will show you how a tight string carries sound.

You will need:

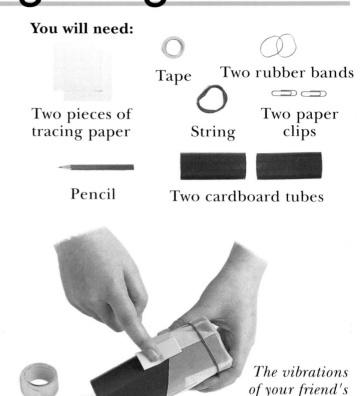

Tape

Two rubber bands

Two pieces of tracing paper

String

Two paper clips

Pencil

Two cardboard tubes

1 Fold a piece of tracing paper over one end of each tube. Attach it with a rubber band.

2 Pull the paper tight and tape it securely.

The vibrations of your friend's voice make the tube and string vibrate.

3 Make a small hole in the center of both pieces of tracing paper.

The vibrating string makes your tube vibrate. You hear those vibrations as your friend's voice.

4 Thread the string through the holes in both tubes. Tie a paper clip to each end to prevent the string from slipping back through the hole.

The vibrations travel swiftly along the tight string. The sound stops if the string is loose and cannot vibrate.

5 Use the tubes as a simple telephone. Hold one tube to your ear and listen while your friend speaks softly into the other tube.

Prong notes
Tapping the prongs of a tuning fork produces a soft musical note. But if you place the handle of the tuning fork on a hard surface, the note becomes louder. The vibrations of the fork travel into the surface, making it vibrate, too.

Finding the beat

Can you hear a sound as faint as a heartbeat? By making a simple stethoscope you will find out how to make soft sounds louder.

You will need:

Scissors

Plastic tubing

Tape

Funnel

1 Insert the funnel into the plastic tube and secure it with tape.

Sound waves from the heart collect in the funnel. They travel along the tube to your ear.

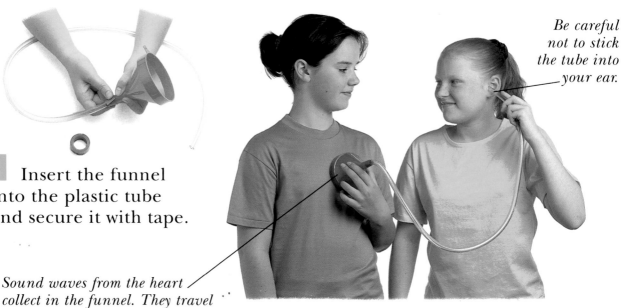

Be careful not to stick the tube into your ear.

2 ⚠ Put the funnel against a friend's chest and hold the end of the tube to your ear. You will hear the low thud of the heart beating.

Listening in

The stethoscopes doctors use have two tubes that allow them to use both ears to listen to sounds inside the body. The sounds they hear tell them whether or not parts of the body are working properly.

Loud mouth

Can you make your voice louder without shouting? With just a sheet of paper and some tape, you can make a megaphone.

You will need:

Tape

Scissors

Large sheet of paper

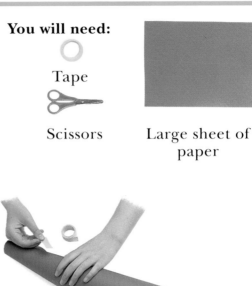

1 Roll the paper into a cone.

2 Tape the edge of the rolled paper to secure it.

The cone collects the sound waves of your voice and sends them forward.

3 Talk into the narrow end of the cone. Your voice sounds louder.

The cone now collects sounds and directs them to your ear.

4 Now place the narrow end of the cone against your ear. You can hear soft sounds much more easily.

Bouncing sound

Sometimes sound waves hit an object before they reach our ears. When this happens, the sound waves bounce back and we hear the sound as a reflection, or "echo." This experiment shows you how to bounce sound.

You will need:

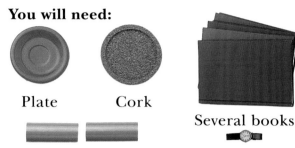

Plate   Cork   Several books

Two cardboard tubes   Watch that ticks

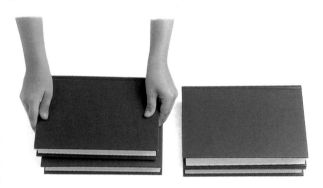

1 Stack two piles of books. They must be the same height.

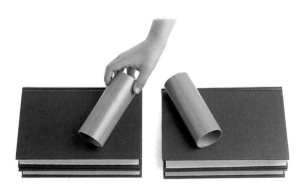

2 Carefully lay the tubes on the books as shown above.

3 Make sure that the watch is ticking.

4 Place the watch just inside the **end of one** tube.

5 Listen at the end of the other tube. You cannot hear the watch. Ask a friend to hold the plate near the far ends of the tubes. Now you can hear the watch.

The sound waves bounce off the plate and travel through the second tube to your ear.

Sound waves from the watch travel through the first tube.

The soft cork soaks up the sound waves.

More things to try
Try pieces of wood, metal, or cotton. Hard surfaces bounce sound, but soft surfaces do not.

6 Replace the plate with the cork. Now you cannot hear the watch.

"Seeing" with sound
When they fly, bats make high squeaking sounds that bounce off objects in their path. These echoes tell the bats about the size and position of objects and allow them to find their way in the dark and catch flying insects.

Plastic drum

How do musical instruments make sounds? Make a drum and see how to change its "pitch," or make the sound higher or lower.

You will need:

Rubber band

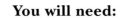

Pen

Sheet of plastic

Plastic bowl

The skin of the drum and the air inside it vibrate to create a booming sound.

1 Fit the plastic over the bowl. Pull the plastic tight and secure it with the rubber band.

2 Grip the plastic firmly to stretch it smoothly across the bowl. Strike it with the pen. It makes the sound of a drum.

Tighten and relax your grip as you play. The note becomes higher and lower. The tighter the skin, the higher the pitch.

Talking drum
The cords on this African drum change its pitch. Pressing them while striking the drum raises and lowers the pitch and produces sounds similar to someone talking.

Simple shakers

Different percussion instruments produce various noises as you beat or shake them. You can make some shakers and see how different objects create sounds of different pitch.

You will need:

Scissors

Plastic bottle

Colored tape

Paper clips

Make sure the bottle is dry inside.

1 Put a few paper clips into the bottle. Screw on the cap firmly.

Pasta

Dried peas

Pins

Uncooked rice

Marbles

Mustard seeds

Lentils

2 Hold the bottle and shake it back and forth. The paper clips strike the sides of the bottle and produce a rattling sound.

Shake with short flicks of the wrist.

3 Collect other small objects and make more shakers with them. They all make different sounds.

4 You can also decorate your shakers with strips of colored tape.

Rubber guitar

Can you make music with rubber bands? By stretching the bands across a baking pan and plucking them, you can mimic the sound of a guitar and learn how string instruments work.

You will need:

Three coloring pens

Baking pan

Rubber bands of varying thickness

1 Stretch the rubber bands lengthwise across the pan.

2 Pluck the bands. They make a dull sound.

The vibrations of the bands are muffled because they rub against the top of the pan.

The pens raise the rubber bands above the pan.

3 Now put a pen underneath the rubber bands at each end of the pan.

The pitch of the notes depends on how fast the bands vibrate. Thin bands vibrate quickly and produce high notes.

4 Pluck the bands again. The sound is much clearer than it was before.

Thick, heavy bands vibrate less quickly and produce low notes.

Vibrations pass through the pens to the pan. Most of the sound comes from the pan as it vibrates.

5 Press the third pen onto the bands. Slide it back and forth while you pluck the bands. The pitch of the notes changes.

The notes get higher as you shorten the vibrating part of each band.

String sounds
Guitar players press the strings with one hand and pluck them with the other. Pressing the strings changes the notes by making the vibrating parts shorter or longer.

Bottle pipes

You can make music with a few bottles and some water. See and hear how different amounts of air vibrate and make different sounds.

You will need:

Food coloring

Water

Narrow-necked glass bottles

1 Set the bottles in a line. You will need six or more bottles to make a tune.

Gradually change the level of water in each bottle.

2 Pour a different amount of water into each bottle.

3 Color the water to make the levels easier to see.

4 Blow gently across the top of each bottle. Each one produces a different musical note.

Blowing across the top of the bottle makes the air inside vibrate. Short columns of air vibrate more quickly than long columns of air.

You can change the water levels to create different notes and make a tune.

A short column of air makes a high note.

A long column of air makes a low note.

Pipe organ
Each pipe in this huge organ sounds one note. When the organ is played, air is blown across holes at the base of each pipe, causing the column of air in the pipe to vibrate and produce a note. Together, these notes form music.

Cardboard flute

Woodwind instruments, such as the flute, clarinet, and oboe, are pipes with holes in them. With just one cardboard tube you can make your own woodwind instrument that produces several notes.

You will need:

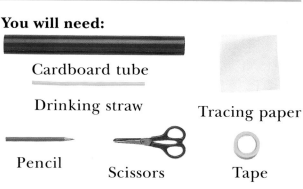

Cardboard tube

Drinking straw

Tracing paper

Pencil

Scissors

Tape

1 Press one end of the straw flat. Cut the sides to make a point.

2 Fold the tracing paper over one end of the tube and secure it with tape.

3 Using the pencil, make a small hole in the center of the tracing paper.

4 Carefully push the round end of the straw through the hole.

The straw vibrates and sends a vibrating column of air down the tube as far as the first uncovered hole, where the air escapes.

5 With the pencil, make six holes along the length of the tube.

6 Cover the holes with your fingers and blow into the straw. By moving your fingers on and off the holes, you can change the pitch of the note.

The longer the column of air, the lower the note.

Bags of sound

To play the bagpipes, the player squeezes the bag, sending air into the pipes. The pipe with holes, or the "chanter," plays a tune. The other pipes each sound only one note.

Picture credits
(Abbreviation key: B=below, C=center, L=left, R=right, T=top)

Catherine Ashmore: 25BL; Clive Barda: 9BL; Dorling Kindersley: 22BL; Pete Gardner: 6BL, 6BR, 7CL, 11BR, 17BR; Robert Harding Picture Library: 13BL; The Image Bank: 15BL; Dave King: 6TL; NHPA/Trureo Nakamuta: 6CR; Stephen Dalton: 21BR; Science Photo Library/ Alexander Tsiaras: 7TL; Chris Priest &

Mark Clarke: 18BL; Scottish Tourist Board: 29CL; Zefa: 27BL

Picture research Paula Cassidy and Rupert Thomas

Production Louise Barratt

Dorling Kindersley would like to thank Claire Gillard for editorial assistance; Mrs Bradbury, the staff and children of Allfarthing Junior School, Wandsworth,

especially Idris Anjary, Melanie Best, Benny Grebot, Miriam Habtesellasse, Alistair Lambert, Lucy Martin, Paul Nolan, Dorothy Opong, Alan Penfold, Ben Saunders, David Tross, and Alice Watling; Tom Armstrong, Michael Brown, Damien Francis, Stacey Higgs, Mela Macgregor, Katie Martin, Susanna Scott, Natasha Shepherd, and Victoria Watling.